THREE
BROTHERS

Thomas Power Lowry, MD

HISTORY BOOKS BY THE AUTHOR

Idle Winter Press
Portland, Oregon
http://IdleWinter.com

This edition published 2017
Printed in the United States of America
The text of this book is in Alegreya

ISBN-13: 978-1945687044 (Idle Winter Press)
ISBN-10: 1945687045

THREE
BROTHERS
Death and Love
in the Civil War

Thomas Power Lowry, MD

Idle Winter Press
Portland, Oregon

CONTENTS

ACKNOWLEDGEMENTS

Beverly A. Lowry, long-time wife, friend, companion, and co-researcher, for her encouragement and fearless proofreading. The Rev. Dr. Albert H. Ledoux, always a guiding light in family and genealogical records research. Robert K. Krick for all things Confederate. Julie Krick for her cartographic skills. The Somerset Historical Center for keeping the flame of history alive. And five generations who preserved the family records.

INTRODUCTION

Can three letters, penned 156 years ago, shed useful light on our nation's history? The answer, almost certainly, is "yes." Just as a paleontologist can say much about a dinosaur from just a few bones, so can historical analysis produce a further addition to the vast corpus of Civil War writing, all starting with those three letters. Here are the people involved, with an exposition of the geography, the political events of the day, the style of romantic correspondence, the ongoing fervor of Christian schisms, and a few terms unfamiliar to today's readers.

Dramatis Personae

The matriarch of the principals was Sarah Myer, born in southwest Pennsylvania around 1820 into a farming family of modest means. In the 1830s, she married Michael Lowry. They had five children: Emanuel Lowry, born 1837, Michael Conrad Lowry, born 1839, and three other children, Maria, Samuel, and Anna. After her husband died, Sarah remarried to a 45-year German immigrant. With John Suhre (also spelled Shure and Suhrie) she gave birth to John Suhre in 1841, Johanna Suhre in 1845, and George Suhre in 1848. In the 1850s her second husband died; she remained a widow.

Religion

Beginning with Martin Luther and John Calvin, Western Christianity moved ever-farther from the Roman Catholic Church. In the United States, this division reached its zenith with the Know Nothing political party, which advocated the exclusion of Catholic immigrants. North America remained almost exclusively Protestant, but the meaning of that term became ever more confusing, as evangelical movements originating in England and Scotland were swiftly transplanted to the New World.

Waves of evangelistic fervor took their form in the First Great Awakening that swept northern Europe and the American colonies in the 1730s and 1740s, with an emphasis on a personal relationship with Christ, and a rejection of ritual and hierarchy. This greatly irritated the more traditional Protestants. The Second Great Awakening, beginning around 1800, introduced increased fervor with "outpourings of the Holy Spirit," manifested by visible excitement and vocalization. This second movement embraced everyone, regardless of age, gender, race, and social status, and made major inroads into the beliefs of blacks, both slave and free. A series of revivals continued over the next century, with the founding of many new branches of Christianity: Mormonism (1820), Seventh-Day Adventism (1863), and Jehovah's Witnesses (1884).

Emanuel Lowry was deeply involved in the reform movement founded by Thomas Campbell (1763-1854) and continued by his son Alexander Campbell (1788-1866). Thomas was born in County Down, now Northern Ireland. Though raised as an Anglican, he was ordained a minister in the Scottish Seceder Presbyterian Church around1790. Shortly after his 1807 arrival in America he parted ways with other Presbyterian groups over doctrinal matters. After a brief association with the immersion Baptists, Campbell founded the Disciples of Christ, emphasizing primitive Christianity and rejecting anything not specifically mentioned in Scripture, such as musical instruments in worship. Thomas Campbell founded Bethany College, which continues today, in 1840. His son Alexander carried on his father's work and was still a vivid presence during Emanuel's stay in Bethany. Emanuel paid his way through college by his work on the *Millennial Harbinger*, a monthly publication devoted to reconciliation between Protestant groups, so that they would be better prepared for the Second Coming of Jesus Christ. Around 1850, the editorship was assumed by W. K. Pendleton who almost certainly was Emanuel's work supervisor.

The Campbell movement continues to flourish as a major Christian denomination under its current name, The Christian Church (Disciples of Christ). The author's grandmother, Chloe Simms Lowry, was a major supporter of the church in Oakland, California, using her husband's money to replace the seating and install a large stained-glass window, visible even today.

The author's grandmother was certainly not the best-known member of The Christian Church (Disciples). Other include: Edgar Cayce (prophet and mysticist); J. William Fulbright (senator); David Lloyd George (prime minister); Ben Hogan (golfer); Lyndon

B. Johnson (president); John Muir (naturalist); Col. Harlan Sanders (KFC); Tom Selleck (actor); John Stamos (actor); Lew Wallace (author of *Ben Hur*); and John Wooden (basketball coach).

Another member, more of notoriety than fame, was Jim Jones, charismatic church leader, the first man to murder a sitting US Congressman, and instigator of the Guyana massacre carried out by drinking cyanide-laced Kool Aid, acts which clearly violated the precepts of his childhood religious upbringing.

Who's Who & What's What

The Civil War is a distant country, inhabited by historians, re-enactors, and heritage buffs, but to Emanuel Lowry and his brothers it was present reality, his here and now. His letters contain names and events familiar to nearly every American in 1861, but since some of today's readers may have dozed off during their American history classes, here is some background.

"Seward." William H. Seward was Lincoln's Secretary of State. He strongly opposed slavery, but cared even more about preserving the Union. As Southern fire-eaters urged their followers toward open secession, Seward worked desperately to forge a compromise which would preserve the country, undivided. With Lincoln's approval, Seward proposed an amendment that would guarantee slavery forever in the slave states, but prohibit its spread to the western territories. Protecting slavery forever seems like a desperate measure today, but the 1860s were desperate times. The compromise pleased no one. The slave states demanded the right to fill New Mexico and Arizona with slaves. The northern Radical Republicans wanted to abolish slavery everywhere. Seward's long and illustrious career could fill a book and, indeed, has filled several.

"Greeley." Horace Greeley was the founder and editor of the *New York Tribune*, one of the most influential newspapers in American history. His long career included an 1859 trip across the United States by stagecoach (remember—no railroad) during which his adventures included the first press interview of Brigham Young. Greeley's trip inspired his famous suggestion of "Go west, young man." In politics, he supported Lincoln (with major exceptions) and began the 1860s favoring compromise with the South. This soon turned to burning anti-slavery sentiment and demand for immediate military action to crush the new Confederacy. One staffer coined the "On to Richmond" slogan. While Seward worked for compromise. Greeley favored force.

"Missouri Compromise." No summary can possibly do justice to this issue but the underlying theme is that the slave states feared being out numbered in the US Senate by the free states. This issue was less complex when the United States were mostly clustered on the Atlantic seaboard, but two enormous acquisitions of territory, the Louisiana Purchase (1803) and the entire southwest, seized from Mexico in 1848, raised the stakes. The Missouri Compromise of 1820 admitted Missouri as a slave state and Maine as a free state. In addition, slavery was forbidden north of the 36 degrees, 30 minutes parallel (excluding Missouri) and Arkansas Territory (later Arkansas, Indian Territory, and Oklahoma) would be a slave territory. This avoided war until 1848, when the South wanted slavery extended into what is now New Mexico and Arizona. The Wilmot Proviso (1846) proposed banning slavery in all territory seized from Mexico, but was defeated by senators from the slave states. What followed was the Missouri Compromise of 1850, in which Texas gave up its claims to New Mexico, California was admitted as a free state, sales of slaves in the District of Columbia were stopped, and the fugitive slave laws were strengthened. This only delayed the impending crisis. A last-minute attempt to avoid war came in the Crittenden Compromise of 1860. This would forbid slavery forever north of the 36' 30" line, forbid Federal interference in interstate slave trade, and provide Federal compensation to owners of slaves who escaped. Neither North nor South approved this compromise.

"Nullification" is the legal theory that the states can "nullify" any Federal law that the state believes is unconstitutional. The first major event involving nullification involved the state of Georgia stealing the land of the Cherokee nation. The US Supreme Court ruled against Georgia, which ignored that decision. In the years before the Civil War the greatest proponent of nullification was Senator John C. Calhoun of South Carolina, who objected to much of the legislation which emanated from the north. No Federal court has ever upheld nullification.

"Fire eater." This term refers to the editors and politicians, mostly Southern, whose speeches, editorials, and beliefs were angry, inflammatory, and unsusceptible to compromise.

"Chirography" is a technical term for handwriting (*chiros* hand + *graphos* writing). In the centuries of cursive usage, writing "a fine hand" was considered a virtue. In the era of texting, the flying thumbs on a smartphone have nullified an ancient art.

With this brief background, we proceed to the letter of Emanuel Lowry to his brother, almost certainly Michael Conrad Lowry, written just sixty days before open warfare broke out between the United

States and the Confederacy. Emanuel's words are full of deep fear and hopeful solutions.

CHAPTER 1
TERRA COGNITA

The southwest quadrant of Pennsylvania and the adjacent "finger" of West Virginia are quiet backwaters today, but they were very familiar to the Lowry and Suhre clans 150 years ago. For the benefit of today's readers, here is a thumbnail sketch of eight of the locations mentioned in these three letters, with their current populations. As an indication of their economies today, the author has attached the percentage of the population of each which is currently living below the most recent definition of poverty: a family of four living on less than $23,850 per annum. For comparison, sixteen percent of Californians are below the poverty level. The map will give a sense of their relative locations.

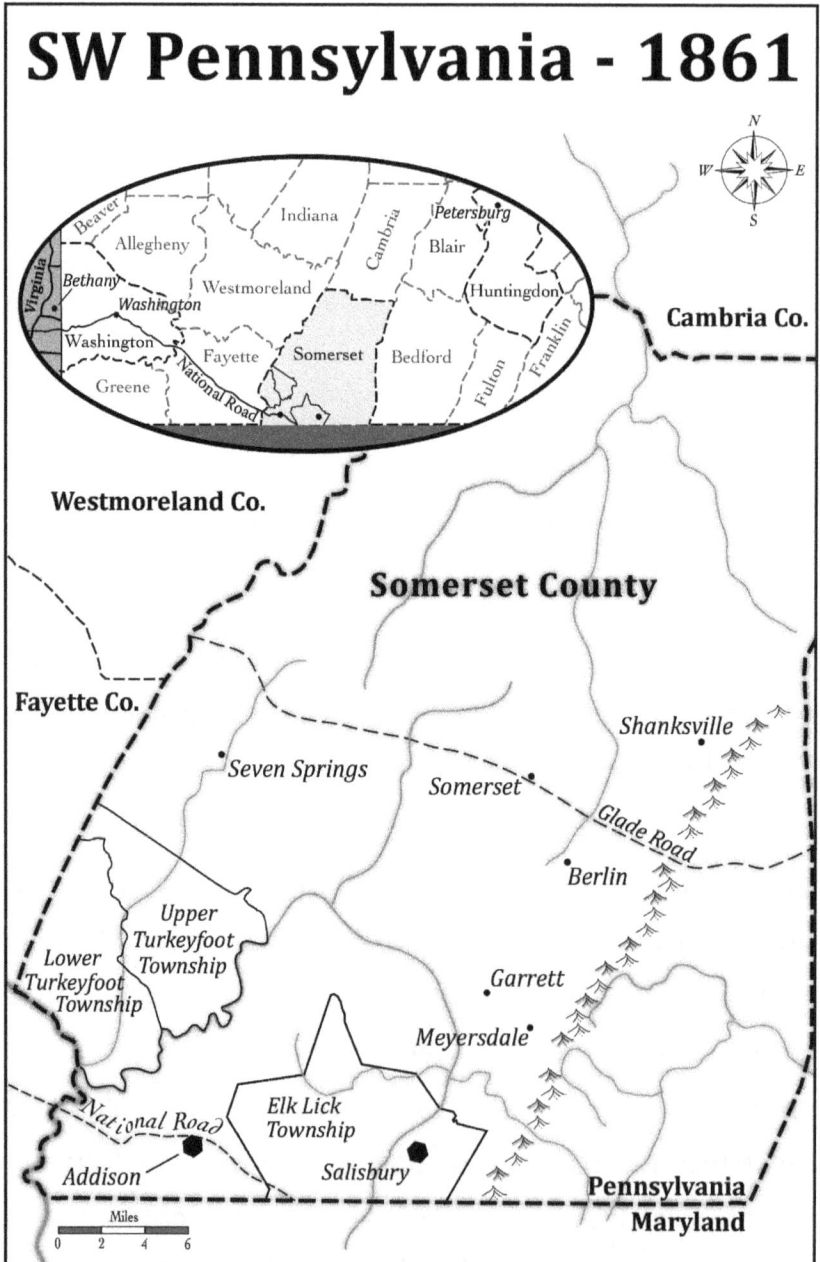

SW Pennsylvania - 1861

Addison was founded in 1798. It was on the Old National Road, and still contains the Petersburg Tollhouse. Today's population is 207, with 14% in poverty;

Bethany, WV, had 335 inhabitants in 1880. Today it has a population of 1,036, with 11% in poverty.

Elk Lick Township, population 2,200, with 14% in poverty. Its claim to fame is Mount Davis, highest point in Pennsylvania.

Petersburg, in Huntingdon County, on the Little Juniata River, was a stop on the Pennsylvania Railroad Line. Population in 1860 334; 455 today. Poverty 6%.

Salisbury, population 727, with unknown percent in poverty, was founded in 1794 on Turkeyfoot Road.

Turkeyfoot Township, Upper, appears in a hand-drawn map made by George Washington in 1754. Three convergent rivers formed a "turkeyfoot." Current population 1,200, with 10% in poverty.

Turkeyfoot Township, Lower, was the site of the Jersey Baptist Church. Current population 672, with 18% in poverty.

Washington was settled in 1768. Many were immigrants from Scotland and Northern Ireland. Current population 14,000, with 21% in poverty.

In 1860, Somerset County, Pennsylvania had a population of 27,080. Today that figure is near 80,000.

In 1860, Brooke County, (West) Virginia had a population of 5,500. Today's population is near 24,000, with 12% in poverty.

CHAPTER 2

EMANUEL WRITES TO HIS BROTHER

Bethany, Brooke Co., Va.

Feb. 20, 1861

My Dear Brother:

My last letter was written in a state of almost total physical and mental prostration, when all my powers were crying out for rest, and every nerve protested against the least exertion of mind. That will account for its deficiencies. I suppose you could tell, even from the chirography, that there was something wrong. I must confess that I wrote in perfect ignorance of the true nature of the Crittenden Proposition of Compromise, which I had never read, and which I

29

supposed merely extended the Missouri line to the Pacific. Being induced to examine it more closely by the persist refusal of the leading Republicans to entertain what I considered so simple and just a proposition, I was amazed to find out its true character and of course agree with you that the Republicans can never agree to it. Neither will it be necessary; for if the border States once become convinced that they cannot get that they will be satisfied with less.

Your reply to my letter was just such as I had anticipated; and I am very far from agreeing with you in all your positions, believing that their adoption by the Republican party would inevitably cover it with eternal infamy, by making it the author of one of the fiercest and bloodiest war on the rolls of time. That is, if you stand on the Tribune platform, as your letter seems to indicate. Now listen, dear brother, you sneer at Seward, etc., for talking of Compromise, what else is there to be done. The Gulf States are in open rebellion, and of course we make no concession to compromise with them. But here are the border States, just trembling in the balance, <u>which will follow their Southern Sisters just as certain as day follows night unless we grant them some concession.</u> This is the plain blunt fact that stares me in the face. They will be satisfied with a recognition of their right to take their slaves into the territories just the same as their horses. <u>This we have no right to refuse them</u>; for the constitution, as expounded by the highest tribunal in the land, gives them the privilege. And while this is the law of the land we must obey it, no matter how much it is repugnant to our individual principles and higher law-isms; else what right have <u>we</u> to talk of nullification and secession?! It will be a barren right to them, at most, for I don't suppose they would ever be able to plant slavery permanently into any [of] our present territories. But if we, Greeley-like, stand back on our dignity, and refuse to agree to this just and exceedingly simple mode of settlement, what will be the result [?]. We must either attempt the desperate step of forcing a united South into terms by the sword, or retire peaceably to our side of Mason & Dixon's line, giving them all their territory, and making a treaty with them of perpetual peace and amity. There is the alternative; how do you like it. Pooh! says Greeley, we have a government; we will soon whip the rebels into traces. Ah! There is the dreadful mistake; the mistake of infatuation. Dear brother, if the idea has ever entered into any unguarded segment of your brain by reason of thought, or been borne to you on wings of imagination, or startled you in the silent hours of the night by appearing as one of the magic elements of a dream, that we can <u>whip</u> the south back into its allegiance, banish the monstrous element at once from all the chambers of your mind, as a deadly thing, not to be entertained for a moment. If we grant to the border states the concessions, or rather rights, I have indicated, they will stand firm, and the seceding States <u>must of necessity</u> come back. If we do not [do] so, we array the South against us in solid column, and idea of being able to <u>conquer</u> them is the sheerest nonsense that ever entered into the brain even of fanaticism. <u>We cannot do it</u>. It is utterly impossible. Not even with England and France to do it. Weigh well the solemn words of Macauley, "Woe to the government that cannot distinguish between a nation and a mob." Therefore a war is not to thought of. For after 20 years' fighting we would be no nearer our goal than now, and with the whole wealth and prosperity of both sections destroyed, we'd have at last to make an ignominious peace.

Rest assured the public sentiment of the North is rather with Seward the conservative than with Greeley the fanatic. So will "Old Abe" be, unless he is more infatuated than I give him credit for. Recollect, a compromise we <u>must</u> have, or a separation is inevitable. The Southern traitors of course dread nothing so much as a compromise on which the Border States could stand; for in that event they know very well their jig would be up; and every refusal of the Republicans to agree to terms of adjustment is hailed by them with most lively joy. Restoration of the Missouri Compromise line, and extension to the Pacific, is about as much as the Republicans can grant, and with this I think the border States would be satisfied. If not, the only course left is separation; but let it be peaceable, for it is utter nonsense to talk of one section whipping the other. A war under the circumstances would be the most gigantic mistake ever made, and would inevitably subject its authors to the everlasting execration of mankind. And such a war! What mortal imagination can conceive of the awful horrors attending it! Rather than such a consummation be brought upon us, let the requiem of the Republican party be sung by the waves of oblivion. God grant that wise and moderate counsels may prevail. Of course, it is the duty of the President to hold all U.S. property, even at the point of the sword, until the question becomes settled, or until required by treaty to surrender it. Such, dear brother, is my view of these matters, reasoning from all the premises. Subsequent events may alter these views very materially. Don't suppose that I so unqualifiedly oppose a coercive policy from any fear or cowardice, or recreancy [sic] to my principles—or that I wouldn't heartily endorse this way of settling the matter, as the most proper, if there was any possible hope of gaining the object desired. I oppose it only because of my firm conviction that it would be wasting blood and treasure in vain. I perfectly agree with Greeley& Co. in the correctness of the theory of coercion in cases of this kind. But when it is most clearly evident to everyone that takes the trouble to think it all about the matter, that the revolted provinces cannot by any possibility be conquered, any more than could the colonies in 1776, why then it is madness to attempt to carry the theory into practice. Two ways are then open for the settlement of our difficulties and only two, in the minds of reasonable men —viz: either to compromise, or allow the South to retire peaceably and form a government of their own—a mighty republic by the side of ours—slave—while ours will be free. Which do you prefer? If the latter, do not blame Seward, etc., or myself, for preferring the former, as long as there is hope of realizing it without sacrificing too much, and thus endeavoring to preserve our glorious country in unity.

But perhaps I have written too much on this subject already. Your letter came to hand last night and I need not assure you was received with very great pleasure, as usual. I hope you attended the wedding and had a good time. I have been attending several parties here—one of them Prof. Pendleton's, and one at Mr.

Campbell's house—the former a general affair, to
which all the students were invited, and which passed
off very pleasantly with a splendid supper, excellent
music by the young ladies, etc.—the latter an affair got
up by the students to welcome Mr. Campbell home after an absence of two months in Indiana on a finan-
cing tour for the College. Passed off Do. [sic] with an
oyster supper. Everything is quiet here now. The secessionist have collapsed completely since their over-
whelming defeat on the delegate election. Pickett was
beat almost two to one, at which the students were
duly exasperated but could not help themselves. I rep-
resented Prof. Pendleton as a secessionist. I am not
able positively to say whether he is or not, tho' that
seems to be the general impression. It is hard to get at
his real opinions. Two of my chums have left—the Gar-
vin brothers—one to teach school in O. the other to
prosecute his studies at Miami University. Therefore
Shuff & I constitute the family and are getting along
fine. Six of the Free State students have left, including
Benson, and the worst fire-eaters, so that conservatism
and peace now shed their benignant light over us.

I suppose your school is verging to a close; and
earnestly hope you will have no difficulty in getting
into a good situation immediately thereafter. My plans
have suffered no change, and if our unhappy national

difficulties are peacefully settled, I see nothing in the way of their consummation. (I verily believe my chirography is getting worse every day, while yours is getting better.)

What is Sam going to do the coming year? Will he stay in the Dehave [?] house? I wrote a letter to Fanny just one week before my last to you, to which I received no reply. Please tell her so, and to "hurry up the cakes." My love to mother and the rest, while I remain in the bonds of changeless affection. Your brother, Emanuel Lowrey [sic].

Postlude

Emanuel wrote to his brother, Michael Conrad Lowry, on February 20, 1861. On April 12, 1861, the Confederates fired on Fort Sumter. On April 24, 1861, Michael joined the 10th Regiment of the Pennsylvania Reserve Corps. Events were running far ahead of Emanuel's predictions.

On June 7, 1862, at Gaines Mill, Michael was seriously wounded in the thigh. In a remarkable stroke of fortune for later biographers, he was wounded with Pvt. Andrew Roy, Company A, 10th Pennsylvania Reserves. Roy, a man of remarkable memory and clear expository prose told us much about "M. C. [Michael

Conrad] Lowry," in his 1909 *Recollections of a Prisoner of War.*

Roy and Lowry had many conversations with their captors, both as they lay untended on the battle-field and later in Richmond's infamous tobacco ware-house prison. Roy and Lowry became close comrades in their months as prisoners. Here, mostly para-phrased, are Roy's observations. Discussing the war with their more intelligent captors, Michael informed them "frankly but kindly" that the war would not be over until the seceded states returned to the fold. On another occasion, a Southerner of some importance as-serted that any Southern man would know more about Chesterfield (English earl, widely read author on how to be a gentleman) in five minutes than any Yankee in a lifetime. Michael retorted, "I have not found all Southerners gentlemen and I'm damned if I'm talking to a gentleman now." The self-important rebel backed away. Roy's wound, seven inches long, exposing the shattered bone, soon swarmed with maggots. Michael sharpened a stick and extracted hundreds of maggots but they returned over and over again. To distract his patient from this disgusting procedure he sang all the verses of "Annie Laurie" over and over again.

Once off the trampled ground that comprised the rebel "hospital," Roy arrived, with 163 other men, on the third floor of the tobacco warehouse, whose floor held three inches of dried tobacco juice. This was the mattress for all the men. Lowry was on the second floor, with similar accommodations. He came upstairs frequently (Roy was too crippled to reciprocate.) On one visit, Lowry asked Roy what he thought of the prison. Roy compared it with the stanzas in Milton's *Paradise Lost*, citing Satan's soliloquy after being hurled into the bottomless pit, the verse beginning, "Farewell, happy fields; hail, horrors; hail." Lowry replied, "All right, but you must remember that Satan was never confined in a tobacco warehouse, in the Capital of the Confederacy; otherwise he would not have been so courageous and self-contained. Well, we must make the best of it we can for, as Shakespeare says: 'Things are never at worst So long as we can say: 'This is the worst.'"

One day, Michael again climbed the stairs, bearing a great smile and a newspaper. In it was printed an eleven-stanza poem on Napoleon, by Lord Byron. "Roy, I have just finished reading it. Let us memorize it. You can have the paper for an hour, then I will call for it and keep it for an hour; we will exchange the paper every hour until we have the poem memorized, and see who comes out victor." Lowry was the winner, reciting it all from memory; Roy was still struggling with the final stanza.

In his memoirs, Roy cites the difference between American and European armies; in the latter, the soldiers are ignorant and illiterate, taught only to obey. "The privates among the [American] volunteers were in many cases better educated and more intelligent than the officers who commanded them." He cited as an example, his comrade Lowry, "who possessed the elements of a general, and would have risen to high command if his life [had been] spared, frequently discussed the errors and defects of McClellan's generalship ... he insisted that McClellan should have attacked Lee when the rebel army was divided, with a river between the two wings."

Roy's final communication from Lowry came as the latter was a convalescent at Camp Parole. That last letter contained a prediction that Maj. Gen. John Pope, newly appointed to high command, would not last long. He was right; the arrogant and pompous Pope was soon in disgrace. Michael Conrad Lowry would have one final encounter with incompetent high command.

Four months later, he was well enough to return to his regiment. In late October, he sent money to his mother, urging her to use it "for comforts." Two months later, his regiment was part of Gen. William Franklin's left wing in the attack on Fredericksburg. In an a poorly managed attack, Michael and his comrades splashed through a dreadful swamp, under heavy artillery fire, and climbed the slopes as far as the Confederate trenches. The Union high command failed to support this breakthrough. More than 1,800 Pennsylvania troops were killed before the survivors retreated. Michael was one of the dead. His body was never identified. From Roy's memoirs, we saw that Michael was a great loss to his country. Well-educated, thoughtful, intelligent, and brave. Although only a teacher in the common schools of a rural county, his knowledge of literature, as well as military strategy, far exceeded that found in most college graduates today.

One part of Emanuel's predictions certainly came true. There was terrible shedding of blood. He had lost two brothers in one battle. And the war was barely begun.

CHAPTER 3

EMANUEL WRITES TO HIS FIANCÉ

Prelude

In the following letter, Emanuel writes to his intended bride. But what do we know about her? In 1850, the United State Census taker passed through Turkeyfoot Township, Somerset County, Pennsylvania. The thirty-fifth family in his collection was headed by Sylvester (Silvester) Colburn, aged 56, born "about 1794," in Pennsylvania. In the household with him were Sarah (age 26), David (age 23), Mary (age 18), Silvester (age 15), Phebe (age 13), Ann (age 10), Louisa (age 2), and John (age six months). Other records suggest that *pater familias* Sylvester married three times and sired a total of twenty-six children. In 1850, his wife, Olive, seems to be the mother of all these children. Was motherhood with Silvester exhausting unto death? When Emanuel wrote to Phebe (later Phoebe), she was age twenty-four, teaching school at Addison. He lifted his pen and wrote:

Bethany, Brooke Co., Va., May 30, 1861

My Dear Phebe.

Once a week! Yes, that was it: if I sympathized with you while at Petersburg, I would write to you at least once a week. I will not promise absolutely to do all that; for sometimes I can't write anything, of the simplest kind, for a week or two, but there is nothing to hinder me from writing to you today; nothing to keep back the free heart that goes out on the wings of fancy, wearing garlands of sweetest flowers to crown your brow. Addison is in a South-eastern direction from this, and the distance from here to Petersburg by way of the national road is about eighty miles. How easy it would be for me to go to Washington, (Pa.) take the hack and be with you in twenty-four hours. Wouldn't it. And how many times, and in what alluring shapes and guises, does the temptation present itself. O! to feel your heart beating against mine once more again, and your kiss of sweetest affection trembling on my lips—that were happiness worth longing for, worth enduring for. An eventful year has this been that is soon to roll into the shadowy realms of the past. Eventful in many respects. Eventful to me chiefly in giving me enlarged and worthier view of life, its duties and responsibilities, its higher and nobler objects—sadly eventful, too, in showing me the hollowness and worthlessness of all human institutions and professions.

But all this has only driven me to my own heart and caused me to value more highly its treasures—strengthening, deepening, and purifying its affections, and—but where am I going? I was just going to tell you, Phebe, what language fails to tell, even when whispered in tones of of softest harmony, and in strains of magic eloquence—what can only be told by the mute glance of the eye, lit with love's holiest light, by the soft pressure of the hand, when silence seals the lips, and the heart struggles with mighty waves of tenderness—it's very chambers overflowing with exquisite harmonies.

To Addison I cannot go, for several good and sufficient reasons—chief of which is, that I cannot leave the office at present. So I must content myself with the varied dreams of anticipations, and try to get bread out of the stones of this model town. Salisbury used to be my pattern of selfishness, dullness, and apathy, but Salisbury, compared with Bethany, is a paradise of sociability and life. But Bethany is not to blame; it only happens not to have the right kind of people to command respect. But this don't trouble me, as I am not one of the Bethanyites, though among them. Between the thoughts, tastes, feelings, sentiments, and education of myself and the majority of them, there is a gulf almost as wide as that between DRIES?? And LAPONS??.

Yet it has a few redeeming features. There is one man here, and <u>only</u> one, (besides "the Bishop") whom I profoundly respect and love—James A. Campbell, the confidential clerk and agent of A. C., and my employer in the printing office. Everybody loves him; everybody respects him. On his open brow nature stamped the indelible impress of her own patent of nobility. The earnest, conscientious and high-souled Christian, patriot and <u>man</u>—he is a necessary figure in the moral landscape of Bethany, to prevent its complete envelopment in the most profound gloom. Another figure I will point out to you before long.

What a fine thing it is to be ignorant and how I dislike it to tear away the vail [sic] that hides an unwelcome sight from the eyes of a fellow-creature. But these people called Disciples, spread all over this fair land are certainly the subjects of a most marvelous illusion in regards to this paradise of Bethany, and its famed college. Well, it may be charity not to say much about the latter institution, as it is now in a trough of the sea, tossed and rocked by the huge billows, in danger of being hurled to the bottom at any moment, never more to rise again. And I feel almost indifferent about its fate, for it is useless to conceal the fact that during the last two years, at least, its management has been a gigantic farce—a simple mockery. And if it is to rise from the sea in renovated strength, only to be placed under the same management, it will be better, I believe if the waves swallow it up. In the meantime, my own boat again lies stranded high and dry on the timeless sand; and it is needless to say that in the fate of Bethany College my own is in a great measure bound up. But I am not in the least concerned in the future, having not in vain schooled myself for the important lesson that "Sufficient unto the day is the evil thereof."

Dear Phebe, perhaps you think I am only amusing myself, drawing fancy sketches, and following the wild lead of the siren, imagination. But, it is not so. These are the calm and matured thoughts and reflections of months of intimate aquaintanceship [sic] with Bethany and Beth. Coll.; and because they are so, I talk of them indifferently, and almost with levity. Heavy scales have fallen from my eyes during the last eight months; and were I to tell you the half of what I have learned, it would take you a month to get over your astonishment. So I will put off telling you any more until I can do so in a less tedious manner than this—with this arm that now guides the pen around your waist, and your hand pressed in mine, while zephyrs from the wings of the angels of love are playing about us.

But I know just what you are thinking about, what part is Prof. Loos playing in this drama? Ah, you Somerset folks have also set up an idol which may eventually prove nothing but a hundred others of the same kind. Far be it from me to say anything derogatory to the character and standing of Prof. Loos, for I owe him much, and know well that he stands too high for me to be a judge of his motives and actions. But a few thoughts and opinions I can give you—for I am talking to you in confidence, and as I would talk to no human being besides—as if I were talking only to my own heart. I am far from satisfied with course of the Professor, and I have abundant reasons. In the classroom he is everything we could wish, but that is all. Once out of that, he appears to be oblivious of any such institutions as Bethany College, or place as Bethany.— immersed in his books or thoughts—content to leave all management in the hands of Mr. Pendleton. Once only did he condescend to preach for us this winter, though there is always such an anxiety to hear him by the people, wearied of the everlasting repetitions of the Bishop, and the platitudes of Messrs. Pendleton and Pickett.

In one word, he seems to regard us all with the utmost indifference, and as a natural consequence, he comes to be regarded in the same way. You say you like him better than ever for his course in the present crisis. I beg leave to differ with you. In a crisis like this, it is <u>impossible</u> for a man to remain neutral, and retain the respect of anybody. You know that much of human nature yourself, Phebe, and of universal experience. It is only men of bold, firm and decided opinions that can influence the people. Your wishy-washy, milk-and-water men, who attempt to carry water on both shoulders never do anything. And the effects of Loos's non-commital policy are already apparent. He belongs to neither party, and both regard him with distrust and suspicion. So he is losing respect on all sides, and rapidly sinking to a cypher in the community, a man without influence. How different James Campbell! A bold and unflinching Union man from the start, he has battled energetically for the cause, without in the least compromising his Christian character—and there is not now a man in the place more universally respected, or who wields a greater influence.

Of course I do not desire a Christian minister to bring these matters into the pulpit (just the contrary) or to spend any part of his time loudly proclaiming his sentiments, but in a grave crisis like this, where every man is watched and weighed, he must let his neighbors know where he stands, or her cannot retain influence. He cannot be on good terms with either side if both regard him with suspicion; but if he boldly takes his stand on one side or the other he can easily command the respect of both, if he is the right kind of man. With Franklin it is another matter, as he is travelling continually, and has nothing to do but preach. But I do not pretend to judge Loos's motives; and he is very probably in the right and I in the wrong, and things will all come out right yet. At least, take these remarks only for speculation.

But verily, it lacks two days of a week since I mailed my last, and I think I ought to keep this back that long. Still, as it's about done I may as well let it go. I think I have given you some food for thought until you get my next. And so, as ever, Faithfully yours,

Emanuel Lowrey [sic].

ORIGINAL.

"Thou wilt think of me."

HELEN A. BROWN.

When other forms are round thee,
  In other, happy hours,
And other joys have bound thee,
  Their festal wreath of flow'rs.

When other smiles are dancing,
  In mirthfulness and glee
And other eyes are glancing,
  So full of light, to thee.

When music-tones are ringing,
  A vesper-symphony,
And Memory is bringing,
  Her visions back to thee.

Oh! let some thrilling measure,
  Some floating, heart-felt strain,
Awake some banished pleasure,
  Some olden joy again.

Then mid those forms around thee
  Those other scenes of glee,
Where festal joys have crowned thee
  I know thou 'lt think of me.

Miss Inez Colborn,
Athens,
Somerset County,
State of Penna

Postlude

This letter can be analyzed in two dimensions: style and content. As to style, the editor, although wishing to be proud of his ancestor's self-presentation, found himself silently screaming, "Immanuel, get on with it!" Emanuel is the un-Hemingway, seemingly unable to write concise narrative prose, trapped in an ooze of indirection, analogy, simile, metaphor, and innuendo. In the course of reading 75,000 Civil War military trial transcripts, with hundreds of attached letters and depositions, the author has never encountered prose as pointlessly convoluted as the above. A review of the content may prove more fruitful.

His brother, Michael Conrad Lowry, had enlisted in the army four weeks earlier, exposing himself, of course, to the horrors of war. Of Michael—not a word. All across the country was ferment and violent passions. Bethany was in Virginia. On April 4, 1861, a Virginia state convention voted against secession. On April 12, the Confederates opened fire on Union-held Fort Sumter. Two days later, Lincoln called up troops to put down the rebellion. The Virginia convention then took a new vote and went for secession. The western counties of Virginia had little in common with the slave-holding counties of tidewater Virginia and convened the First Wheeling Convention, May 13-15, 1861, to discuss the formation of West Virginia.

These momentous events, splitting a nation and splitting Virginia itself, occupied every newspaper. The telegraph wires buzzed with hour by hour updates, yet Emanuel seemed fixed on his emotions regarding certain professors and the ways in which they fell short of his expectations. Although he remained a devoted life-long member of The Christian Church (Disciples) he was deeply disenchanted with Bethany and Bethany College, at least during his stay there.

How to account for these seeming contradiction and omissions? Any answer would be speculation, but a few possibilities emerge. Perhaps daily events were so ever present that there was no need to comment upon them. Another possibility is one that Freud much later made salient. Emanuel comes across as cranky and irritable. He is age twenty-four and apparently in good health. He is many miles from his intended bride. His early pages are suffused with, "your heart beating against mine," "kiss of sweetest affection trembling on my lips," and "garlands of sweetest flowers." In the Victorian era, "self abuse" was regarded not only as a sin but also as a cause of premature death. Perhaps his ancient mammalian physiology collided with his ideals of Christian purity, the result being a vague annoyance at nearly everything around him. What is clear is that in the midst of a national crisis his expressed thoughts were narrow, limited, sad, and largely domestic.

One of Emanuel's *betes noir* was Professor Charles L. Loos. A glance at the 1860 US census returns sheds interesting light. He is listed as "Professor of Ancient Languages." Perhaps Loos saw our impending Civil War as a replay of the Peloponnesian War, when ancient Sparta and Athens destroyed each other in years of foolish attempts to dominate the Mediterranean. Or perhaps he was distracted by his wife, his sons, ages 10, 9, and 6, and his daughters, ages 7, 4, 2, and 3 months.

In spite of Emanuel's gloomy mien in 1861, his life was only beginning. On September 24, 1862, at Somerset, Pennsylvania, he and Phoebe were united in marriage. (Other sources say the marriage was in Elk Lick Township, Somerset County.) For the next ten years, they lived at Bethany, West Virginia, where Emanuel continued his affiliation with Bethany College. In 1872, they moved to Eureka, Illinois. In 1875, they settled, for the rest of their lives, in Gibson City, Illinois. He was soon editor of the *Gibson City Courier*, a post he held until 1897, when "paralysis agitans" (probably Parkinson's Disease) forced him to retire. From then, until his death in 1907, Phoebe tended to his every need. She followed him in death the next year, felled by typhoid fever. Their published obituaries emphasized Christian virtues and public service.

Bethany

A Small College of National Distinction

They had five children, three born during their years at Bethany. Emily died in 1884. John died in 1900. As of 1908, sons Charles Edward Lowry and James Percival Lowry were living in Gibson City, while Russell was in San Francisco. In 1940, Russell wrote to "Percy" about the same letters reproduced here, praising his father for his "serious thought and reflection—quite a contrast to the flippant and light-hearted youth of today." (See Appendix B) But Russell added that "for all my reverence and admiration, [he] never seemed really close me."

Shelves of novels explore the relationships of fathers and sons. The fragmentary relics reproduced here only hint at the coolness and disappointment in a "normal" and "Christian" household.

CHAPTER 4
LOUISA MAY ALCOTT
AND JOHN SUHRE

John Suhre had a short military career and an
apotheosis a century and a half later. He was mustered
into Capt. Schrock's Company (Company D), 133rd Regiment of Pennsylvania Infantry on August 14, 1862, at
Somerset, Pennsylvania. It was a nine-month enlistment. He never completed those months.

The dry facts of his military service records tell
one version of the story. Other records, by another
hand, will tell us of grief, suffering, and character. The
muster roll for December 1862 notes, "Absent.
Wounded in action December 13 at Fredericksburg, Va.

and sent to hospital." The January-February report tells us, "Died January 1, 1863 of wounds received at Fredericksburg." The mustering out roll of March 1863 seems to contradict part of a previous entry, "Died at Washington DC Dec 1862." A Descriptive List, dated December 28, 1862 spells his name as Suhrie and describes him as, "gray eyes. black hair. fair complexion. 5 feet 9 inches. Occupation blacksmith. Enlisted at Shanksville, Pa. Never paid." Another record, a "Casualty Sheet," states "Died Dec. 26th, 1862."

Yet another record sheet, Record of Death and Interment, states that John died at "Military Hospital, Union Hotel, Georgetown, DC, December 26, 1862, and that "it is desired his remains should be interred with the usual military honors." According to this record, he was buried that same day. Location not stated. That's it —every scrap of information in his Compiled Military Service Record.

Getting shot was not a random event. It began at the very top. Lincoln appointed Gen. Ambrose Burnside as commander of the Army of the Potomac. Burnside said, "I am not fit for so large a command," or words to that effect. The AOTP was huge with a clumsy command structure and no staff to aid Burnside. The center of the fight was Marye's Heights, above Fredericksburg. A stone wall, along a sunken road, shielded hundreds of Confederate riflemen. Above them were ranks of artillery. The Union men marching uphill against this defensive position were mowed down like grass. None ever made it to the first Confederate position. Among the units sent against Robert E. Lee's army were John Suhre's 133rd Pennsylvanians, part of Allabach's Brigade, A. A. Humphrey's Division. In Suhre's regiment alone, twenty men were killed on the field, 145 were wounded (many died shortly afterward), and nineteen were missing. The word "slaughter" barely suffices. (Dyer's *Compendium* lists 44 men killed or mortally wound, and 33 dead of disease for the entire war. The discrepancy remains unexplained.)

Now we know the location of his wounding and the date of his death. Other sources show that he was buried in the cemetery at what is now the Armed Forces Retirement Home, overlooking Washington, DC, the same site as Lincoln's summer cottage. Suhre's tombstone, shown on the back cover, has his name, misspelled. A tree has nudged the stone out of line and its roots embrace the actual burial. In a sense, he is reborn as a tree. But none of this explains Suhre's sudden fame in this era. That arises in the days between his wound and his death, and is a triumph of modern scholarship. But before bringing forth this new insight we must look at the one document we have in Suhre's own hand.

"Camp near Sharpesburgh

Oct, 6th 1862

My Dear Sister.

You will see by the heading of this letter that we are still in vacinaty of Sharpesburgh. i do not know how long we will remain here. Perhaps we will make our winter quarters here. i am so ancious to here from home. It is almost three weeks now or quiet since we got our last mail. i cannot account for this unless it is through the bad management of our officers, but i believe they are trying to make arrangements now to have our letters for warded from Washington. I heard this morning that our mail was on the road. How true it is i am unable to say. i wonder if you receive My letters but i suppose you do. We drew our bounty the other day which was twenty five dollars and two dollars premium, making twenty seven dollars. i will send some of it home the first oppertunity i get. i do not like to risk it in a letter, not until i hear whether my letters reaches you regularly at least. Let me see: i wrote one to Anna, one to Mother, and this one makes three since George sent me those stamps. i sent Mike one dollar. [probably Michael Conrad Lowry] He told me in his last letter that he paid the last three cents to mail it. I told him if he needed any more he should let me know. It is not very pleasant to be out of money altogether. He says there is four or five months coming to him but says he thinks they will not draw any as long as they are kept there. When you write again pleas let me know if Emanuel is at home. I have not written to him yet, it is really a shame but I did not know for the last six weeks where a letter would find him, wether he was at home or still at Bethany. The weather continues to be very warm here through the day but during the night it is rather cooler than necessary to be comfortable. If i would have one of Mother['s] old quilts here it would add to my comfort considerable. We were obliged to leave our wollen Blankets in Washington when we left there but then i think they will be sent after us but the time is almost here to have the lights extinguished so i must close, the captain tells me that we would letter [better] have our letters sent to Hagerstown. Hereafter give my love [to] Mother and all the rest and Remember your Devoted

    John F. Suhre

    Company D

    133 Regt

    Hagerstown MD

    Alaboch's Brigade"

His letter is much like thousands of other soldier's letters. We haven't been paid. No safe way to send money. Hoping for mail. What do the generals have planned? Give my love to mother. There were literally millions of Civil War soldiers. What will lift him out of the crowd? The answer lies in one name: Louisa May Alcott.

Today, she is one of America's best-known authors, particularly for *Little Women* and *Little Men*, as well as several other novels and dozens of short stories. But in November 1862, her literary output was a few short publications of no particular merit. She lived at home with her financially feckless father, who refused to see any merit in his daughter. She was a strong Unionist and abolitionist, and as soon as she turned thirty (the minimum age to be an army nurse) she arrived at the Union Hotel Hospital, Georgetown, District of Columbia. Her first three days there were spent tending medical patients: ",,,pneumonia on one side, diphtheria on the other, and two typhoids opposite...." Then came the wounded from Fredericksburg, forty ambulances full. Any dreams of gentility in nursing vanished as she confronted a ward crowded with mud soaked, vile smelling, disfigured, and mangled men. She set to washing them and bringing food, tea, and medicine until she was exhausted. In her 1863 book, *Hospital*

Sketches, her first literary success, she gave dozens of examples of the courageous suffering of the soldiers, and the horrors of bleeding, draining pus, rotting amputation stumps, and death.

In her narrative, one patient stood out from the rest. She described him as a "Virginia blacksmith," gave his age as thirty, and listed the names of several siblings. She followed his worsening condition as his bullet-shattered lung filled with fluid. She did what the surgeon had not the heart to do: tell him that he could not recover. When she brought him the terrible news, great silent tears rolled down his cheeks. "[I] took him in, as gathering the bent head in my arms, as freely as if he had been a little child, I said 'Let me help you bear it, John.'" She stood in awe of his stoicism. He held her hand in his final agony, drawing comfort that she stayed with him. He became the soul of her hospital memoirs. But who was he? It appears that in her published narrative, *Hospital Sketches*, she falsified many details about "John," but in her private journal, kept during her actual stay at the hospital, she named him as "John Suhre" and later as "John Sulie." However, since her book described him as a Virginian, researchers were thrown off the scent for over a century.

In the author's family papers there was a hint that he might have been John Suhre, but Alcott's many clues seemed to point away. The author's search for connections, twenty years ago, failed to document a connection. In the year 2015, in a brilliant piece of investigative journalism, John Matteson, proved the connection. Professor Matteson (see Appendix D) was no stranger to the Alcotts. His 2008 *Eden's Outcasts: The Story of Louisa May Alcott and Her Father* explored in depth their changing relationship. He then found a key in George C. Rable's 2002 *Fredericksburg! Fredericksburg! The Classic Account of the Battle and Irs Place in Civil War History.* In the chapter on "Wounds," Rable mentioned a letter written from a Georgetown hospital to the mother of a soldier named "John Shure," This led Matteson to the archives of the Army War College, at Carlisle, Pennsylvania. That letter was by Edward Morgan Schrock, Suhre's company commander when he enlisted. In it, Schrock informed John's mother that her son's wounds were fatal. These findings, and some family information at the Historical and Genealogical Society of Somerset County Pennsylvania, confirmed that the mortally wounded John Suhre was indeed Louisa May Alcott's "Prince of Patients."

And what of Louisa May herself? A month after Suhre's death, she herself was desperately ill with typhoid pneumonia. Her father came to get her and just in time; she seemed likely to die on the way home. Once there, she remained in a delirium for months. When she awoke, she was a changed woman, her true literary voice awakened, and a lifetime of literary success open before her.

And what of John Suhre's mortal remains? Louisa May recorded that his comrades and nurses had such deep respect for him that he was allowed to stay in his bed for a few hours, lying in state, as it were, rather than be hustled off to the dead house as was usual. Soon though, he had to go. Within in a day he was buried at what is now the United States Soldier's and Airmen's Home National Cemetery, where he rests today.

CHAPTER 5

THE WIDOW SARAH

_____

Our first consideration is the form of the evidence. For 150 years her pension application was saved, first by the War Department, then since 1934 in the National Archives. Around five years ago her application was digitized by a commercial firm, Fold3. The original records are no longer available to the public. The digitized version is too blurry to be reproduced as illustrations, therefore what appears here are transcripts of the imperfect Fold3 images.

Before displaying the contents of the application itself, what is startling in the records is that she signed with an "X." In 1860, only 6.2% of white Pennsylvania women were illiterate and she was one of them. Which makes the literacy of her sons, two of whom, Emanuel and Samuel, became newspaper editors, quite remarkable. Another son, Michael, could quote Shakespeare, Milton, and Byron from memory. Quite a jump from one generation to the next.

The first, and most informative, document is a blank government form entitled "WIDOWED MOTHERS ARMY PENSION." It has a series of open spaces to be filled in by the applicant. In Sarah's case, another hand filled in the blanks as she was illiterate. In the following typescript, the material inserted in the blanks is presented in italics.

State of *Pennsylvania.* City of *Somerset.* SS.

On this *28th* day of *July* AD one thousand eight hundred and sixty *three* personally appeared before me *W. H. Koontz Prothonotary of the Court of Common Pleas of Somerset County Pennsylvania. Sarah Suhrie* [sic] a resident of *Elklick* in the County of *Somerset* and State of *Pennsylvania* aged *56* years, who being first duly sworn, according to law, doth on her oath make the following declaration, in order to obtain the benefits of the provision made by the act of Congress approved July 14th, 1862: That she is the widow of   *Joseph Suhrie, being previously married* [to] *Michael Lowry,*   and mother of   *Michael Lowry*   who was a   *private*   in company   *A*   commanded by *Capt. J. S. Hinckman*   [later killed at Second Bull Run] In the   *10th*   regiment of   *the Pennsylvania Reserve Corps*   in the war of 1861, who   *was killed at the battle of Fredericksburg Virginia on the 13th of December 1862.*

She further declares that her said son, upon whom she was wholly or in part dependent for support, having left no widow or minor child under sixteen years of age surviving, declarant makes this application for a pension under the above mentioned act, and refers to the evidence filed herewith, and that in the proper department to establish her claim. She also declares that she has not, in any way, been engaged in, or aided, or abetted, the rebellion in the United States; that she is not in receipt of a pension under the 2nd section of the act above mentioned, or any other act, nor has she again married since the death of her son, the said *Michael C. Lowry*   deceased.

She further states that she was married to Michael Lowry in the year 1824 who died in 1839 that she was subsequently married to Joseph Suhrie in the year 1841 who died in 1856 that her maiden name was Meyer [nearly illegible] and she hereby appoints *Henry F. Scholl* her true and lawful attorney, with full power of substitution to present and prosecute this her claim for Pension, and to receive and receipt for any order or certificate that may be issued in satisfaction thereof.

her
Sarah X Suhrie
Mark

Sworn to and subscribed and the power of attorney duly acknowledged before me, the day and year above written, and I hereby certify that I have no interest, direct or indirect, in the prosecution of this claim.
W. H. Koontz Prothonotary

The next page in Sarah's file is another fill-in-the-blank form, this one headed, in capital letters, "WAR OF 1861." As before, the printed sections are in normal font, while hand -written entries are in italics.

Brief in the case of *Mrs. Sarah Suhrie, mother of Michael C. Lowry, private Co. A, 10 Pa. R.C. Somerset* County, and State of *Penn.* Act of July 14, 1862. Post Office address of Applicant, *Elklick, Somerset Co., Pa.* Claim for *Widow's* Pension.

Declarations and Identifications in due Form
PROOF EXHIBITED

Muster in July 21, 1861 and killed in battle Dec. 13, 1862 from the Rolls. Widowhood and identification shown by the usual testimony. Relationship and [illegible] *shown by the affidavits of credible witnesses. Powers of atty. In due form.*

Admitted *Mar. 31, 186* [illegible] to a Pension of $8.00 per month, commencing *Dec. 13,* 1862. *Henry F. School Esq. Somerset, Pa. W.S. Graff* Examining Clerk.

Another page, entirely handwritten and often illegible, reads as follows:

———————————

State of Pennsylvania County of Somerset. Sarah Suhrie, being duly affirmed according to law says that she was married to Michael Lowry in the year 1824 by Peter Rhodes, Esq. at Shanksville, Pa., that in the year 1839 her said husband died, that in the year 1841 she was married to Joseph Suhrie by the Rev.—Meyers at Mount Savage, Md,; that he died in the year 1856. She further states that there is no record evidence of her marriages and that owing to the lapse of time and removal of the persons who [illegible] and those present at the weddings she is unable to tell where they are or whether they are living or not. She further states that Michael C. Lowry of Co A 19ᵗʰ Regt P.R.V.C. deceased was her son by her first husband.

———————————

Here, Sarah signed with her customary "X."
At the bottom of the page is inscribed:

———————————

Affirmed and   [illegible]   before me this first day of August, 1863, and I certify that the witness is reputable and

entitled to credit and that I have no interest in the prosecution
of this claim. Sam. Mier, J.P

(Mount Savage is a town in Allegany County, Maryland, only a few miles south of Pennsylvania. Shortly after the time of her wedding there, the town became a major iron and coal center, one of the few places in the country able to produce full-size iron railroad track. Today it has a population of 873. A few of the streets are still paved with cobblestones.)

Yet another handwritten document is in Sarah's pension file. It, too, is often illegible.

State of Pennsylvania Somerset County. I W.H. Koontz
Prothonotary of the Court of Common Pleas of Somerset
County, Penna. Do hereby certify that Saml Mier Esq. before
whom the foregoing affidavits were made was at the time of so
doing an Acting Justice of the Peace in and for said county
duly commissioned [illegible] *official acts as such due*
faith are and of right ought to be given and that the
signatures thereto are genuine & that I have no interest in this
claim. In Testimony whereof I have herewith set my hand

and affix my official seal at Somerset this 5 Aug 1863. W. H. Koontz Prothonotary.

In the Index of Wills of Somerset County for 1879 Sarah Suhrie, who died at Salisbury, we see that her will was probated 11 November 1879. The will itself was filed in Volume Six, Page 167. The will itself begins with the usual legal preliminaries. The relevant portion is as follows.

"1.   I hereby do give and bequeath to my beloved daughter Maria Lowry in fee simple and full ownership without any liens whatever all my properties real and personal including all my effects of any kind and nature.

2.   I hereby intentionally omit to make any bequests to any of my other children or grandchildren because they are better provided for in [illegible] goods than my said daughter Maria who has taken care of me in my age and because it is the expressed wish of all my other children that all my [illegible] be left to said daughter Maria.

3.   I hereby appoint George Lowry and Samuel Lowry the executors of this my last will and testament."

CHAPTER 6

CONCLUSIONS

As this small book was reaching completion, the past returned to bite the present—at Charlottesville, Virginia. In a rally, announced weeks earlier as "Unite the Right," an assortment of neo-Nazis, neo-Confederates, Ku Klux Klansmen, alt-righters, white supremacists, and a self-appointed "militia" armed with AR-15s, came to "protect" a Confederate monument just outside the gates of the University of Virginia. The date was August 12, 2017.

This drew a wide assortment of counter-protesters, many of whom were relatively benign liberals.

However, their numbers were supplemented with adherents to Black Lives Matter and members of Antifa, a sinister, masked, black-garbed "anti-fascist" group with a taste for self-righteous violence. Both sides arrived with sticks, clubs, and pepper spray, while the right-wing group added flaming tiki torches to their arsenal. The police failed to either disarm or separate the two factions. There were deaths and many serious injuries. The blaming and investigations went on for months afterward. The issues of the Civil War are still with us. How does this fatal scuffle relate to the story of the Lowry and Suhre families?

Here the author confesses to three biases: he is a physician, he is a Northerner, and he is a descendant. The first year of medical school included one thousand hours dissecting a corpse. There are no random or unnecessary parts in the human corpus; the "only a shoulder wound" of the cinema could only be portrayed by someone who has never had a wound in the complex of structures that fills the shoulder. Further studies in pathology and neuropathology added very specific details to the nature of injury. Swelling, tearing, ripping, and bleeding, followed by infection, pus, and rotting flesh. The specifics of the 600,000+ men who died in that conflict has removed from the author any sense of romance or any of the glamor purveyed by many history buffs. True there was courage, but in no sense is war noble.

My second bias is that of a Northerner, not a New England Yankee but a California Northerner. In my growing up there I saw little or no interest in the Civil War. Living history had passed it by. My great-uncle and maternal grandfather were World War One veterans. My father and both uncles wore uniforms in the Second World War. California built ships and airplanes and raised huge crops. Our history was the Gold Rush, the Donner Party, and Hollywood. Later, living in Virginia, I discovered just under the surface, a still burning sense of resentment, anger, and bitterness. Southern honor had been tarnished by the surrender at Appomattox. Somehow, the Yankees had cheated and won unfairly. All Heaven must be offended by such cosmic injustice. Yankee bankers, abolitionists, and carpetbaggers were merely slave stealers. John Suhre and Michael Conrad Lowry hardly fit that pattern, one a blacksmith, the other a schoolteacher, not the capitalist conspirators invoked by inflammatory Southern editors. The Southern response might be: "You just don't understand." And, indeed, I don't.

As for my family, emerging from the mists of old documents, we see the widow Sarah with three grown sons. Two are dead at Fredericksburg, while the third is a seminary student, with minimal gainful employment. The dead sons had marketable job skills and better-than-average educations, valuable citizens in any country. To support herself and her minor children, the widow was awarded $8.00 a month, roughly $240.00 in today's dollars.

It is true that the state-by-state Confederate pension system provided even more poorly, but that hardly lessened the burden of death laid on my own family. The author cannot provide any Toynbee-esque sweeping structure or formula, nor can he interpret the inscrutable ways of the Almighty, but can there be any conclusion other than the obvious: most wars are more costly than the issues they are supposed to settle?

THE APOTHEOSIS OF CHIROGRAPHY

Emanuel Lowry probably wrote hundreds, maybe thousands, of letters in his lifetime. The two that came down through often-neglected family papers appear early in this work. Facsimiles of the first pages of the two letters will be displayed shortly. Their like will never be seen again. There are many reasons.

When the author was in school, penmanship was mandatory. There were examinations. There were grades There was still the concept of "writing a fine hand." Each desk at Frank C. Havens Grammar School had a special hole for holding an inkwell, each with its own cork. We were issued wooden pen holders with steel nibs. We learned to dip the pen the proper depth. Too much ink and a great blot appeared on the page. Not enough ink and the pen went dry after writing a single word. After mastering these hydraulics, we were then to shape our letters following the Palmer Method. There were little songs to guide the shapes, especially of the capital letters. The only one the author can recall is the one which sent the boys into gales of suppressed giggles: "One, two, three. Swing your P."

Try as I might, I could not form the beautiful script achieved by most of the girls and a few of the boys. In the fifth-grade my teacher took me aside and confided in me. "Tomorrow the state inspector for the Palmer Method is coming to evaluate my work in teaching penmanship. Your writing is so awful that it will affect my grade. Please stay home tomorrow." I did.

Now many schools have stopped teaching cursive writing. Lovers communicate by tweets and texts and Instagrams. There will no historic record. Here is what Emanuel left us.

But before despair engulfs the lovers of artisanal penmanship, a cheer for graduates of Oregon's Reed College, most of whom master a calligraphic style of writing, and in the world of the Civil War, we see the fine hand of the legendary archivist, Michael P. Musick, whose artistry appears below. We inquired from whence he learned his craft. The ever-modest polymath replied," I have to admit I'm not really a calligrapher. I just picked up an ordinary writing exercise book from the 1850s and tried to duplicate what was in it."

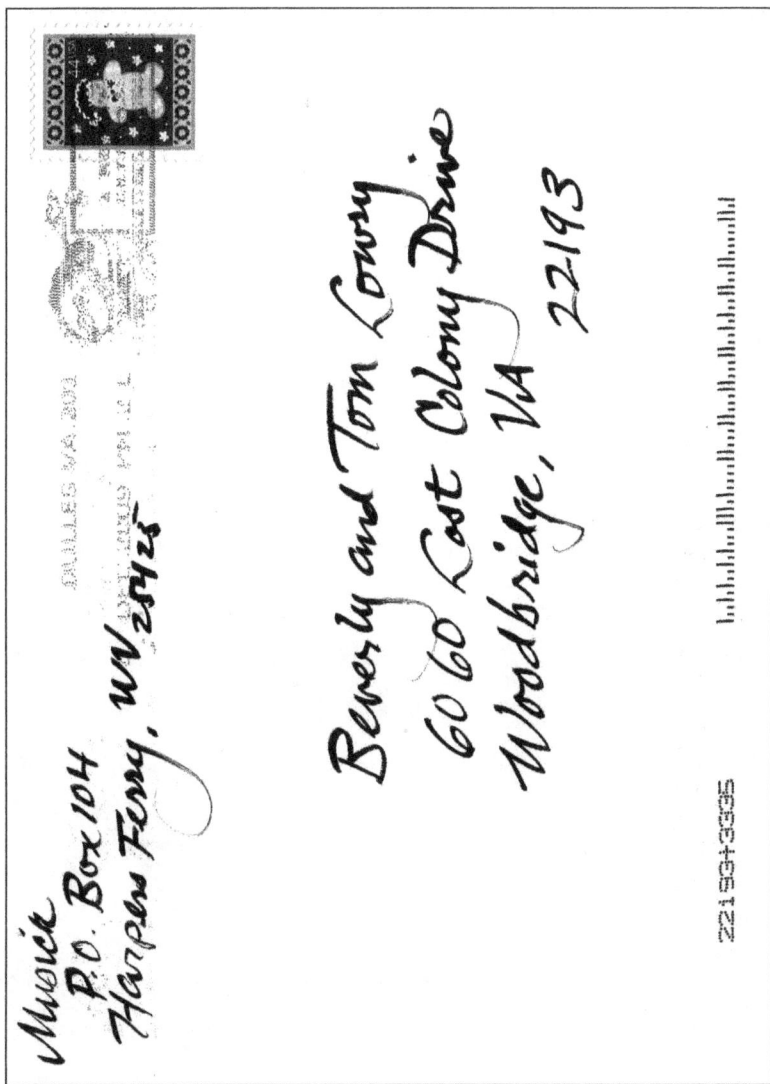

The handwriting of Emanuel Lowry may lack the
flourishes and arabesques of the calligraphic style, but
nearly every word is clearly shaped and easily readable.

Bethany, Brook co., Va., May 30/61.

My dear Phebe!

Once a week! Yes, that
was it: if I sympathized with you while
at Petersburg, I would write to you at
least once a week. I will not promise absolutely to do all that, for sometimes I can't
write any thing, of the simplest kind, for a
week or two, but there is nothing to hinder me
from writing to you to-day; nothing to keep
back the free heart that goes out on the wings
of fancy, wearing garlands of sweetest flowers,
to crown your brow. Addison is in a south-eastern direction from this, and the distance
from here to Petersburg by way of the national
road is about eighty miles. How easy, it would
be for me to go to Washington (Pa.) take the hack,
and be with you in twenty-four hours. Wouldn't
it. And how many times, and in what alluring
shapes and guises, does the temptation present
itself. O, to feel your heart beating against mine
once more again, and your kiss of purest affection

RUSSELL LOWRY
WRITES OF HIS FATHER

"665 Vernon Street, Oakland [California]

Sunday, January seven-1940

Dear Percy [James Percival Lowry]:

Recently there came into my possession a letter [the one from Emanuel to his brother] which I am passing on to you. It was written by your father—and mine—nearly seventy-nine years ago, and his view at that time was very interesting. Less than three months afterward the Civil War was to begin, changing profoundly the course of life for all Americans. Six southern states had already seceded and desperate efforts were being made to find some ground of agreement that might avert the impending hostilities so dreaded by both sides to the controversy. Illustrating again how men can be in the grip of blind forces beyond their power to control, sweeping them on to the consequences, quite outside the scope of reason, expectation or desire. The Crittenden Proposition of Compromise, to which the letter refers, , was one of those methods by which Senator Crittenden of Kentucky, himself a slaveholder, sought to ensure the preservation of the Union without violating the essential principles so deeply held by both the North and the South. The Proposition failed to carry and preparations for war went on.

Aside from the evidence of serious thought and reflection upon the vital political issues of the day—quite a contrast to the flippant and light-hearted attitude of youth in our day—the correspondence is interesting to me for its flawless English composition and fine chirography, and the pathetic reference to his "state of almost total physical and mental prostration, when all my powers were crying out for rest, and every nerve protested against the least exertion of mind." And he was only twenty-four years old, I believe, at the time. It must have been later, then, that mother came along with her exuberant vitality and buoyant disposition to help him over the rough places.

Helen Spalding picked up this letter, with other ancient family documents, when she was in Pennsylvania last summer, and gave it to me just a few days ago. I send it to you because of our common interest, and the belief that it will interest you as it did me. It reveals a personality that, for all my reverence and admiration, never seemed really close to me.

Our belated rains finally have arrived, to cheer the hearts of farmers and stockmen. It is raining like the dickens at this very moment. All the family are as well as usual, and send their love. Affectionately your brother, *Russell*"

The author was too young to remember much of this grandfather, mostly a memory of a kindly old man in bed dying, but he left a legacy of two children, Emily and Richard, and a 40-year banking career, in which he headed the Central National Bank of Oakland, which issued its own currency. (In the years 1865-1935, certain banks with proven reserves could arrange with the Treasury Department to add the word "National" to their name and issue their own currency, so-called "National Currency." Today, such bills are "highly collectable" [valuable] today.)

I do recall being taken into a vault and shown a thousand-dollar bill. He kept a large home library with its own card catalog. In 1926, he was voted onto the

Executive Council of the American Bankers Association. A natural conservative, he drove a gray Packard
Straight-Eight four-door sedan, with no radio or
heater. He considered those to be frivolous.

A PLETHORA OF MICHAEL LOWRYS

The name Michael Lowry appears over many years in southwest Pennsylvania, especially in Somerset County. From entries in the US Census and Findagrave.com a few documented facts emerge.

In files which the author cannot now locate, a Michael Lowry of the United Kingdom was convicted of stealing an iron shovel and was sentenced to be transported to the colonies, arriving in the New World in 1760, if memory serves. (After the American Revolution, transported felons were sent to Australia.)

A Michael Lowry, Sr. died in 1803 and his will was probated at the Somerset County Courthouse May 11, 1803. His son, Michael Lowry, Jr. was born January 3, 1760 in Lancaster, Pennsylvania, and served 1777-1781 in Captain Andrew Porter's Company of Pennsylvania Artillery. He received a pension until his death in September 1833, at Shanksville, Somerset County.

The 1830 US Census at Elk Lick, Somerset County, shows a Michal [sic] Lowry, as head of a household of four "white persons." (Censuses before 1850 showed the name of the head of household but just the ages of the other members.)

The 1880 US Census shows an eight-year old Michael Lowry, of Gay Street, Salisbury. Father was Samuel Lowry, who no doubt named his young son after Samuel's deceased brother, Michael Conrad Lowry.

JOHN MATTESON, SCHOLAR

Louisa May Alcott's literary reputation rests heavily on *Little Women* and *Little Men*, but her first real literary success was *Hospital Sketches*, published in 1863 and republished many times since. In it she described her brief and almost fatal stay as a nurse, encountering the sick and wounded from the Battle of Fredericksburg. A considerable portion of the book is devoted to her favorite patient, a young man who was shot through the lungs and soon died. She was deeply moved by his fortitude in the face of pain and death.

But who was he? Alcott gave many false clues in her book and the matter was a mystery for 150 years. Enter John Matteson, who cracked the code, utilizing newly available data from George C. Rable's book, *Fredericksburg!, Fredericksburg!*, the archives at Carlyle Barracks, and the files of the Somerset Historical Center. He found that her favorite patient was Pvt. John Suhre, Company D, 133rd Pennsylvania Volunteers. (The name is often spelled Suhrie and Shure.)

Matteson is no stranger to the Alcott story. His 2008 book *Eden's Outcasts: The Story of Louisa May Alcott and Her Father* won the Pulitzer Prize for biography. He has written for a considerable variety of publications, including the *New York Times* and the *Wall Street Journal*. His education covers a wide spectrum. His prep years were at the Menlo School in Atherton, California. He received an A.B. in history from Princeton, a J.D. from Harvard Law School, and a Ph.D. in English from Columbia. His legal career included litigation with several firms and a clerkship with a US District Court Judge.

He is currently a professor of English and legal writing at John Jay College of Criminal Justice in New York City.

Clio, the Greek Muse of History

LITERACY IN THE 1860s

Authors need readers. Newspapers need readers. Everyday citizens, if they write letters, need readers. Louisa May Alcott would be unknown today if it were not for the millions who read her books. How literate was the American population in the years of the Civil War? One startling finding in the literacy of the 292 Virginia soldiers who escaped a Union prison camp to join the US Volunteers was this—forty-seven percent could not even sign their own name. Just an "X" scratched on their enlistment papers. Was this indicative of American literacy in general? To answer this, the author turned to the staff of IPUMS (Integrated Public Use Microdata Series) at the University of Minnesota. The US Census of 1860 recorded many things, including the ability to read and write. Here are the percentages of those illiterate, state by state, grouped first by the future states of the Confederacy, then by those who remained in the Union. The data applies only to white males over the age of twenty.

Alabama 9.9%. Florida 7.5%. Georgia 13.2%. Louisiana 7.0 %. Mississippi 6.4%. North Carolina 16.8%. South Carolina 8.6%. Texas 7.5%. Virginia 13.4%. The average for the future Confederacy was 10.5% illiteracy.

Arkansas 13.0%. California 4.2%. Connecticut 3.2%. Delaware 13.3%. Illinois 6.3%. Indiana 6.9%. Iowa 5.1%. Kentucky 12.7%. Maine 2.3%. Maryland 6.9%. Massachusetts 5.4%. Michigan 3.7%. Minnesota 4.8%. Missouri 9.9%. New Hampshire 1.0%. New Jersey 4.7%. New York 4.2%. Ohio 4.1%. Pennsylvania 3.9%. Rhode Island 7.1%. Tennessee 13.5%. Vermont 5.4%. The average for the Union states was 5.8% illiteracy. If the border states are omitted, the Union average is 5.0% illiteracy.

Turning the issue on its head, in even the most benighted state, 80% of the white male population was literate.

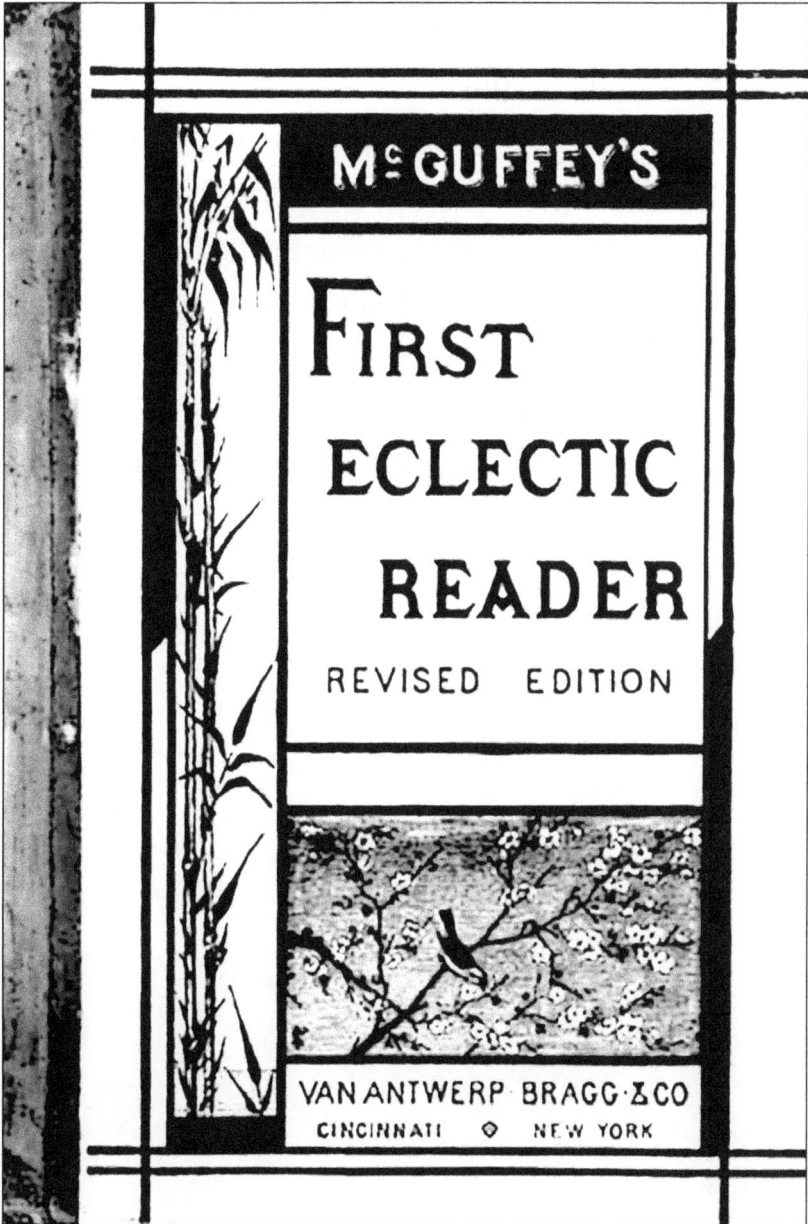

Utah did not have troops in the Civil War, but
their illiteracy rate in 1860 is worth attention: 0.7%—

less than one percent. The founders of the State of Deseret clearly valued education.

How do these figures compare with other parts of the world? In 1850 world-wide 85% of adults could not read or write. In 1860, England had an illiteracy rate of 30%. The English did not begin universal public education until 1870. In France in 1872 33.7% of the population could neither read nor write. With these figures, the United States' efforts at literacy seem quite respectable.

FIVE GENERATIONS ONWARD

One line of descent

Russell
Lowry

Richard S.
Lowry

Thomas P.
Lowry

Shawn T.
Lowry

Megan
Lowry

SOURCES

Alcott, Louisa May: *Hospital Sketches*. 1863. Reprinted by Applewood Books.

Matteson, John: "Finding Private Suhre: On the Trail of Louisa May Alcott's 'Prince of Patients.'" *The New England Quarterly*, vol. LXXXVIII, no. 1 (March 2015).

Roy, Andrew: *Recollections of a Prisoner of War*. Published 1909 by J. L. Trauger Printing, Columbus, Ohio. Reprinted, edited, and annotated in 1996 by William J. Miller, Elliott & Clark Publishing, Montgomery, Alabama, under the title *Fallen Soldier*.

Photo Credits:

John Suhre gravestone: Susan Claffey.

Portrait of Michael Lowry: Somerset Historical Center and Military Images magazine.

Idle
Winter
Press

9 7 8 1 9 4 5 6 8 7 0 4 4